D0757923

In the
Forest

Mary Elizabeth Salzmann

Published by SandCastle™, an imprint of ABDO Publishing Company, 4940 Viking Drive, Edina, Minnesota 55435.

Printed in the United States.

Cover and interior photo credits: Corel, Digital Vision, PhotoDisc.

Library of Congress Cataloging-in-Publication Data

Salzmann, Mary Elizabeth, 1968-
    In the forest / Mary Elizabeth Salzmann.
        p. cm -- (What do you see?)
    ISBN 1-57765-565-6
        1. Forests and forestry--Juvenile literature. [1. Forests and forestry.] I. Title.
    QH86 .S25 2001
    578.73--dc21   2001022016

The SandCastle concept, content, and reading method have been reviewed and approved by a national advisory board including literacy specialists, librarians, elementary school teachers, early childhood education professionals, and parents.

Let Us Know

After reading the book, SandCastle would like you to tell us your stories about reading. What is your favorite page? Was there something hard that you needed help with? Share the ups and downs of learning to read. We want to hear from you! To get posted on the Abdo Publishing Company Web site, send us email at:

sandcastle@abdopub.com

About SandCastle™

Nonfiction books for the beginning reader

- Basic concepts of phonics are incorporated with integrated language methods of reading instruction. Most words are short, and phrases, letter sounds, and word sounds are repeated.

- Readability is determined by the number of words in each sentence, the number of characters in each word, and word lists based on curriculum frameworks.

- Full-color photography reinforces word meanings and concepts.

- "Words I Can Read" list at the end of each book teaches basic elements of grammar, helps the reader recognize the words in the text, and builds vocabulary.

- Reading levels are indicated by the number of flags on the castle.

Look for more SandCastle books in these three reading levels:

Level 1 (one flag)	**Level 2** (two flags)	**Level 3** (three flags)
SandCastle 1	SandCastle 2	SandCastle 3
Grades Pre-K to K 5 or fewer words per page	**Grades K to 1** 5 to 10 words per page	**Grades 1 to 2** 10 to 15 words per page

This is a forest.

Many trees grow in the forest.

Some forests have streams running through them.

This **forest** is growing on a mountain.

Owls live in the forest.

They hunt at night.

This pack of wolves lives in the forest.

Deer live in the forest.

They can run very fast.

This bear is climbing a tree in the forest.

Some tigers live in
forests in Asia.

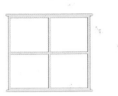

What do you see in this forest?

(skunk)

21

Words I Can Read

Nouns

A noun is a person, place, or thing

bear (BAIR) p. 17
forest (FOR-ist)
  pp. 5, 9, 11, 13, 15, 17, 21
mountain
  (MOUN-tuhn) p. 9

night (NITE) p. 11
pack (PAK) p. 13
skunk (SKUHNGK) p. 21
tree (TREE) p. 17

Plural Nouns

**A plural noun is more than one
person, place, or thing**

deer (DIHR) p. 15
forests (FOR-istss) pp. 7, 19
owls (OULZ) p. 11
streams (STREEMZ) p. 7

tigers (TYE-gurz) p. 19
trees (TREEZ) p. 5
wolves (WULVZ) p. 13

22

Proper Nouns

A proper noun is the name of a person, place, or thing

Asia (AY-zhuh) p. 19

Verbs

A verb is an action or being word

can (KAN) p. 15
climbing (KLIME-ing) p. 17
do (DOO) p. 21
grow (GROH) p. 5
growing (GROH-ing) p. 9
have (HAV) p. 7
hunt (HUHNT) p. 11

is (IZ) pp. 5, 9, 17
live (LIV) pp. 11, 15, 19
lives (LIVZ) p. 13
run (RUHN) p. 15
running (RUHN-ing) p. 7
see (SEE) p. 21

Adjectives

An adjective describes something

many (MEN-ee) p. 5
some (SUHM) pp. 7, 19

this (THISS) pp. 9, 13, 17, 21

What Do You See In the Forest?
Match the Words to the Pictures

deer

owl

trees

wolf